Little Book of Hope

Louise Hall

PEACH PUBLISHING

ISBN 978-1-78036-403-2

Published by

PEACH PUBLISHING

Dedication

This Little Book of Hope is
dedicated to all those in our world who
have lost hard
But loved much
May you rediscover Hope in your heart
and welcome the freedom of joy
back into your lives.

Stay Safe
Stay Strong
Stay True

Our world is a better place
Because of
YOU

Little Book of Hope

Reflections to help guide us through difficult times

Introduction

We are living in a time of great grace. Never before have we been so advanced in science, medicine, research and industry.

We can visit beautiful places on our planet thanks to advances in air, sea, and land travel. And we have access to a multitude of information at our fingertips because of the world wide web.

Some of us have families, others have interesting careers. The young are bright and enthusiastic, and the old are wise and living many more years. We teach and nurture and care and console one another in lots of different ways, each and every day.

The universe is dazzled by the beauty of humanity, and the heavens too must surely smile.

But sometimes, we reach points in our lives, when the ground starts to shift beneath us. We get knocked off course, stumble, fall, and we struggle to get back on our feet.

When this happens, it can be hard to recognise the person staring back in the mirror. We can't see the wood for the trees, and we lose trust in the world, trust in ourselves.

Life is not always a smooth and easy road to travel, and though no one is exempt from troubles, neither are they exempt from love.

There is a light inside us all. When the wind blows hard, it burns low. But once you give it shelter in your heart, soon it will ignite. And no storm will ever fully extinguish it.

This little pocketbook, which you can carry with you wherever you go, is a timely reminder of the gift of Hope that lies inside all of us.

Like all gifts, it should be opened.

'For it is in giving that we
receive.'
St Francis of Assisi

HOPE

Hope….
Where can I find it?
What can it do?
I long to sustain it and show it to you.

My world is now shaken
A thief came in the night
Stole all that is familiar
And put up a fight

Now I stand in the stillness
The door firmly shut
And look through a keyhole
To see a world stuck in a rut

I close my eyes
Behind this locked door
And search for a glimmer
To bring to the fore

Then I see clearly
Something to ignite
It sparkles like diamonds
So clean and so bright

Hope…
I have found it!
Look what it can do!
I'll unlock the door and show it to you

Reflection

I will not try to accomplish
something too big,
for life is made up of precious little
things

You will find richness because
of who you are,
not what you have

Those who have Hope are
healing,
and those who are healed had Hope

Love
And be loved

Be Not Afraid
Where once the storm clouds gathered,
soon a rainbow will replace

Make peace
Keep peace

When there is darkness,
do not complain.

Instead light a candle,
and allow Hope to reign

Remember the value of time
and
the beauty of simplicity

Pick up a fallen friend
and
soothe many sorrows

Hope is a window of opportunity
that encourages you to pull up the blind

In your hands,
hold invisible stones
of prayer, hope, calm and
positivity.

They will be your weapon
against your Goliath

Realise the power of your
hopeful words,
and use them to heal
and to create

Now that the fields are quiet,
you can search for the grains of Hope

Do not worry should you ever misplace
Hope,
for the loss will only ever be temporary

Enlightenment is the positive change
of a hopeful mind

When you think all the ships have sailed,
Hope arrives into your harbour

When your heart dances with desire
inside,
the Hope of fulfilment will always reside

Taking the road less travelled,
often leads to a clearing littered with
Hope

Forgive easily,
both yourself and others,
and you will have many restful nights

Accepting something
as though life has chosen it for you,
will make for a hopeful life

In the winds of change,
Hope finds us new direction
There is a time for everything
The time for Hope is now

On Hope

An open heart becomes a
dwelling place for Hope

It cleanses and purifies the
chambers restoring
vitality within

Then it can help carry
any burden
and soon all the other organs
are cleansed once more

If we choose to knock at Hope,
a door of possibilities opens around us
and we are invited to step in

By sowing the seeds of Hope,
we are sure to enjoy a Spring of rich
bloom

Hope is the beacon of
glimmering light,
out in a darkened sea

Blessed is the wind that carries
Hope on its tails

Allow the hurts of the past to die away,
and the Hopes of the future will survive

A road paved with Hope
leads to destinations of many pleasures

Hope is your antidote to fear

When you are lost in your own desert,
Hope can bring you closer to the oasis,
and water your soul

When you have Hope,
it gives you the confidence
to choose to follow your heart
over your mind

Hope is the chosen armour
of a spiritual warrior

If despair is the colour of scarlet,
Hope is white as snow

Hope leads to commitment.
Commitment to a better life.

Once the commitment is made,
the future is too.

Negative thinking can be reduced
to a myth,
when you believe that Hope is truth

Where God is omnipotent,
Hope is Sovereign

When we choose the path of Hope,
all good things shall be given to us

Hope can save the world
from unnecessary suffering

Through Hope,
you can become
the very best version of yourself

What would a world without Hope be,
but a barren land of dust and dryness

Hope is the light of a promise,
born out of an eternal flame

Hope is like a sharp pencil
- it has a point!

The more Hope we have,
the more we can truly enjoy our lives

To live with Hope,
allows us to trust in a better tomorrow

Hope is not just a feeling,
but a decision and a way of life

Hope brings with it,
the virtues of faith and love.

When we have all three,
they create peace
to help us through the difficult times
in our lives

From Hope,
springs a fountain,
to dampen our sorrows and miseries

Hope brings knowledge and conviction
of a life better served

Do not allow the destruction of Hope in your heart.

It is a precious commodity
bestowed onto you for
safe keeping.

Guard it like you would
a precious jewel

Hope urges us to lead better lives,
so we can embrace and be
fulfilled
with happiness intended for us

When Hope invites you in,
you are welcomed,
regardless of your failings

You will not be troubled by
anything
when you have Hope in your heart

A dose of hope each day is
medicine for the soul

When you house Hope,
you can go visit it any day

Hope awakens and reinstates
the spirituality we were born with
but may have lost along the way

Hope is the beginning
of God's story
About His love for the world

Hope awakens the sleeping heart
to a higher power
who intercedes for us
in our hour of need

When you have Hope,
even the most painful of
sufferings
can become a most beautiful flower of
joy

Hope is beautiful
It is a beauty of the soul

When You Have Hope...

Hope is the bridge that fills the gap
and leads us to a haven

A day with Hope is a day spent in a
garden of tranquillity

When you have Hope,
you have everything –
this truth will set you free

Hope is the Heavens speaking to the
Earth,
telling it of its plan.

The Hope of new inspiration
is dependent on the creative mind

If you choose to fly on the wings of Hope,
you can penetrate any
smokescreen

When God grants you the Hope in your heart,
it is because it aligns with his will for you

Hope is the mantle of consolation
worn over the veil of sadness

The deeper we go into our
journey of Hope,
the closer we get to the center of our
universe

Hope brings a new season of joy
to hearts that have lived through
the harshest of winters

When you have Hope,
it brings a spiritual healing
that is essential for any physical healing

Hope encourages
an active consciousness of God's love
in our day to day lives

Money is not the root of all evil,
greed is.
But Hope is a precious
commodity
that provides a richness of heart

Hope will bring us together once more

The surest bond of a family,
is sealed with the glue of Hope

Nurture the young with Hope,
and they will take good care of the future

Keep company with Hope
and you will never be without a friend

Hope lets the past go
and allows the future to arrive

When you have Hope,
you can cope.

Hope is the gift of trust
that the Heavens bestow unto you

Make hay while the spring sun shines,
and Hope for plenty come fall

Encouragement inspires
confidence
and stimulates Hope

Hope is the swell in the
treacherous seas
that guides the ship safely to shore

When you are weary,
take rest in the place in your heart
that you have reserved for Hope

The Hope for peace
is the best weapon for war

Hope is the bed that rests the weary
and the tonic that gives them strength

A morning started with Hope
leaves all great things to chance

Nothing is impossible or
unreachable
when you have Hope in your life

Hope is the hammer
that can crush dictatorships
and the nail that holds good leadership
tight

Hope allows you to believe
that it is never too late
to be who you always aspired to be

Great economies steamroll on,
driven by a power engine of Hope

Leave be the old decisions
which cannot be mended,
and Hope for a plan better made

Hope is a strategy that can
spur you into positive action

If at first you don’t succeed,
having Hope will inspire you to try again

In the jigsaw of life
Hope is the core piece

Hope is the safety harness
that brings you to the summit

Patience is a virtue
but having Hope knows that
'This too shall pass'

When you witness the beauty of Hope
It illuminates even the smallest of things

Hope is the friend that you can lean on
just as you stumble and fall

Hope brings our wildest dreams
closer to reality

When you have Hope,
your heart unfolds like a flower
opening to the sun

All good things come to those in hopeful wait

You can lose yourself in a
multitude of hopeful thoughts,
You can find yourself in them too

H.O.P.E

Hold Out for a Perfect Ending

Hope has a recurring dream
that finds you in it

Hope reminds troublesome thoughts
they are not worthy of
your attention

Hope is the training courage receives
so it can win over fear

When you have Hope, you will realise
that you are stronger than you think,
cleverer than you think
and loved more than you'll ever know

Baby steps of Hope,
lead to giant leaps of happiness

With every breakdown
comes a breakthrough

Hope puts no limits
on self-belief

Hope allows you believe
that you are exactly
where God wants you to be

Hope serves a purpose
where worry serves none

Hope can give much rest
to a ruminating mind

When you think you are walking into
battle on your own,
know that Hope has your back

Hope and Fear

Hope bites back at the bark of fear

Hope and a Vaccine

Having Hope will help it work

Hope and Sickness

Warning: Hope is contagious

Hope and Death

It is only until we meet again……

'While there's life, there is Hope'
-Stephen Hawking

Hope and the future

What is for you,
will not pass you by

Hope and Belief

True faith is believing
without fully understanding

Hope and Reward

When we weave a blanket of Hope,
a rich tapestry furnishes our life

Hope and Charity

Giving but not expecting
anything in return
gives Hope that we will
recognise the needs of
the vulnerable
in place of our own personal gain

Hope and Collectiveness

Hope to achieve a common good

Hope and Reform

The greatest politicians
must have the Hope
that they will first reform
themselves

Hope and Humanity

Hope is the food that nourishes the soul

Hope and Singing

'Those who sing, pray twice'
St Augustine

Hope and Staying Apart

Do not worry,
for we will be together again soon

On Rebirth

As we rise like a phoenix from the ashes and
leave behind the images of a world devastated
and low, we remember what got us
through the journey, and
recognise it to be an all essential tool to help
navigate us through this life.

Without it, we cannot sustain.
It is ours to cherish forever more.

It is close.
It is reachable.
It will never truly leave our side.

It is what we now strive for and carry on our person each and every day.

It is HOPE

A poem to comfort loss
Five Angels, God and I

Oh, precious one, why did you go,
And leave my warm embrace?

Oh, loved one dear, the light shone bright,
And led me to God's grace

My tears fall down, my dressing gown,
Already stained with grief

My heart is torn, for you I mourn,
I shake just like a leaf.

Please do not fear, oh loved one dear,
For I must tell you this,

Where I live now, is a wonderful place,
A land of eternal bliss

The day I left my earthly home,
Five angels came to say,

"Oh, precious one, do not be scared,
To journey home today"

In glistening gold, with
transparent wings,
They whispered in my ear,

"It's time to come; your work is done,
Our Lord God needs you near"

And then a blessed melody,
Echoed from up high,

I raised my head towards the light
And saw God in the sky.

With arms outstretched,
he welcomed me,
And told me not to fear,

For I could watch my family,
Every day I spent up here.

He told me every answer,
To every question I ever had.

I understand the reason why,
Right now, you will be sad.

Oh, loved one dear, please listen close,
To what I have to say

You were to me, my everything,
Each moment of every day

And though it will be hard for you,
To let me journey on
Please understand, I'm by your side,
I really am not gone.

So, when you lie in bed at night,
And cry out loud my name.

Please know that I'll come
instantly,
To ease your aching pain

And with me on those nights will be,
Five angels from above,
Together we will comfort you,
And fill you with God's love.

Oh, loved one dear, when it's your time,
To journey up so high,
Please do not fear, for there we'll be,
Five angels, God and I

Author's note on *Five Angels, God and I* poem*:*

This poem of Hope was written some years back to comfort my mother and father after my sister died suddenly at the tender age of twenty-six. As many know, grief tears at your soul and leaves a void in your life. The world seems to shift, and all that was once familiar soon seems strangely out of sync.

My sister, who was born with Down's syndrome, brought much joy into our lives, and our family was devastated by her loss. Almost ten years later, my father passed away after many years living with cancer.

In those intermittent years, he always said that he wasn't afraid to die. When pressed and asked why, my father would smile and simply say:
'Because I know I have someone waiting for me.'

Louise Hall, author

About the Author

Louise Hall lives in the seaside village of Malahide, Co. Dublin on the east coast of Ireland. When her sister died suddenly at aged 26 some years back, she decided to write novels, non-fiction and short stories.

Her publications which have been widely received contain themes of Hope, and her short stories have frequently been shortlisted for many awards.

She has appeared a number of times on radio and TV talk shows regarding her fiction and non-fiction works and has written for numerous newspapers and magazines.

Louise is happily married with three children and lives with their ten year old cockapoo dog, Riley.

Printed in Great Britain
by Amazon

68361326R00059